From GED to PhD

MY JOURNEY TOWARD BECOMING AN *EXTRAORDINARY* WOMAN

From GED to PhD

MY JOURNEY TOWARD BECOMING AN *EXTRAORDINARY* WOMAN

WRITTEN BY

BARBARA V. CRUMP

WITH

YVONNE ROSE

CRUMP BOOK PUBLISHING

Teaneck, New Jersey

From GED to Ph.D.

**MY JOURNEY TOWARD BECOMING
AN *EXTRAORDINARY* WOMAN**

Published by:

Crump Book Publishing
Teaneck, New Jersey
barbaracrump@aol.com

Barbara Crump, Publisher
Spencer Crump, Managing Editor
Quality Press.info, Book Packager

The publication is sold with the understanding that the Publisher is not engaged in rendering legal or other professional services. If legal advice or other expert assistance is required, the services of a competent professional person should be sought.

Copyright © 2022 by Barbara Crump
Print ISBN #: 978-1-0880-2501-7
Ebook ISBN #: 978-1-0880-2504-8
Library of Congress Control Number: 2022900227

DEDICATION

This book is dedicated to my husband, Spencer, my parents, Cleveland and Annie Johnson, my children, grandchildren, and all who provided loving support and never complained throughout my long journey of education. I am forever grateful to my husband for his love, encouragement, and inspiration, especially during the times I almost gave up on education. This book is also dedicated to all the young girls who have feelings of insecurity and no confidence. My journey is to let them know they are beautiful, and they have the power to fulfill their passions and accomplish their dreams by believing in themselves and knowing that through Jesus Christ, all things are possible. I also dedicate this book to all teen mothers who are empowered by their dreams.

From GED to Ph.D.

ACKNOWLEDGMENTS

First, I would like to acknowledge Almighty God, the highest, who gave me the strength, courage, and knowledge to pursue my journey to become an *exceptional woman*. Many people have come into my life for the moment to guide me through my fears. I lack names, but I just want to thank each and every one of you who has touched my soul through my journey. I especially want to thank Rose Liggon, who empowered my light to shine in the sixth grade, and Kathrine Crump-Bolling.

Most of all, I would like to thank my husband, Spencer. Without his love and belief in me, I would not be the person I am today.

From GED to Ph.D.

CONTENTS

PREFACE

I have endured a lot during the more than six decades of my life. The most significant occurrences happened, however, when I pursued my education. During that time, I worked full time, and my husband and I raised three children.

From the moment I decided to embark upon my journey, I experienced numerous challenges, which lasted for more than 36 years, and concluded with me earning a doctorate degree in August 2016, just two months after my 64th birthday.

I wrote my book because I wanted people to understand that they could do anything they put their minds to. We often talk about women who don't aspire, and many of those same women talk about the abuse they have endured. I've been through it all. I was a child raising a child and, at the same time, I suffered physical abuse from my child's father – my ex-husband. Everything changed when, with the help of my family, I moved out of town and, soon after, fell in love with the man who would become my current husband, the father of my three children, and my protector.

Preface

I have spent my entire life wondering why fear was so prevalent in me; I am still trying to discover why. Despite all my years spent pursuing an education, I am still learning about the things in life that can make me a better person and I want other people to know that they should never stop learning. My book is part of my personal learning process. It is helping me to pull everything, good and bad, out of my subconscious. It is helping me to be more secure within myself and, most importantly, as I write my story, I am learning to love myself. ***This is my journey.***

From GED to Ph.D.

INTRODUCTION...
ONLY GOD!!!!

When I heard my name, "Barbara Crump," it startled me. I thought I was dreaming, but then I looked around and I saw a melting pot of beautiful people - male and female of diverse ethnicities, ages, sizes, and shapes. We were all dressed alike in black gowns complemented by red caps with gray tassels - and then I realized that I was, indeed, wide awake and this was my reality.

Then I told myself, *This is not me. This is not the same shy little girl from the country who had so much fear and no confidence from the time she was a child right down to not being able to tie my own shoes.*

I looked around and saw my family – my husband Spencer, our three children, grandchildren, my sisters, brothers, and cousins – that's when reality struck me. *I did it!* The day was August 12, 2017, fifty years after I dropped out of high school, I walked to the stage to accept my doctorate degree. Here I was at the Verizon Center in Washington, DC and I cried tears of joy.

There were several events in my life that had brought tears of joy to my eyes. Receiving my bachelor's degree was the biggest tear-jerker because of the difficulties I had adapting to the academic world. This event was the epitome of all my special occasions, probably because it was thirty-six years in the making. And to be perfectly honest, I knew it would not have happened without the love and encouragement of my dear husband, Spencer. He opened my eyes to a future that, I believe, only God could have planned for me. So, I will proceed to tell you about *my journey.*

However, before I discuss my journey, I need to look at fear, *what is it?* Webster's definition of fear is "An unpleasant emotion caused by the belief that someone or something is dangerous, likely to cause pain, or a threat."

Everything that I did in life involved some element of fear. *Where did my fear come from?* I often wondered if there was a genetic link that caused my fear or if it could be something that just derived from my personal experiences as I grew. Perhaps it was developed through not feeling loved or protected as a young child. *I cannot imagine that would be a cause of my persistent fear, given the love that surrounded me within my parents' household.* As I reflected, I did recall a few occurrences that more than likely could be the root cause of my fear. When feelings of protection, encouragement and love were not present, the fear crept in and occupied my soul, making me think that I was not good enough.

There are still moments when I lack that special feeling of beauty and love within me. A lack of confidence was

3

embedded within my soul. Even though I have gained so much in my life, sometimes I wonder how I completed all my accomplishments without self-confidence. *How was that possible?* All I can say is GOD!

Despite my fears and the hurdles I encountered as I grew up, my life has completely evolved. I am now a Registered Nurse with a Bachelor's Degree in Science, and a Nurse Practitioner. I have a specialty focused on Oncology and I took the Advanced Certification in Oncology and passed the first time, thus completing my Ph.D.

So, here I am, Barbara Crump, Ph.D., the first person from my hometown of Cartersville, Virginia to earn a Doctorate degree and the pride and joy of my family and friends. *Yes, I did it!*

Although victory is mine, I cannot claim to be free of my insecurities or fears, but I do know that I am loved and very capable of accomplishing my goals. Most of all, I have learned that "I can do all things through Christ, who strengthens me." (Philippians 4:13)

PART
ONE

From GED to Ph.D.

Chapter 1

FROM WHENCE I CAME

I entered this universe through a dark canal within my mother's body and, even though I probably wanted to smile at being free, instead, I cried at the top of my lungs. I imagine that, at first sight, I was very much afraid of the world into which I had entered and without the warmth and closeness of my mother's womb, I was totally uncertain about what lay ahead for me. Born Barbara Johnson on June 28, 1953, the second child of Annie Mae and Cleveland Johnson, I soon learned how blessed I would be.

My mother was a young woman married to an older man. She was always quiet, seemingly nervous and fearful of her surroundings, living within her own private world; and she never showed her emotions towards me or my siblings. I think I inherited her tendencies. I realized during my childhood that I always felt less important than others. There was a lingering fear of not knowing who I was and not feeling loved. That feeling is still present at times, as I imagine that everyone else must be smarter, better looking, and more loved. For some unknown reason, I always wondered why I was not confident in who I was, what was wrong with me, or why I thought I was different from the other girls.

When I was growing up, I don't remember my mother's conversations because she didn't have much to say, but whenever she did have a heart-to-heart with us, it was always a conversation of substance. Did she ever say, "I love you" to her children? Not that I can recall. My mother's love was not verbally expressed to us, but we always felt her silent and endearing love. I am not sure if we actually knew the definition of love or if our parents knew what it was to express love, but I do know we were content with the simple things in life and I always had a sense of belonging in our big happy family.

My father was a confident, strong, hard-working man who was employed at the sawmill for minimum wages. He was a master woodcutter and very skilled at carpentry. My father did not have a mortgage because he built our home with his own two hands and then added on rooms as the family grew. When he originally built the house, it started out with just three rooms and then he kept building on to it. At first, it just had the kitchen/living room and two bedrooms - one for my parents and one for the seven children.

Unfortunately, my father never knew his father. His parents were never married, and he was raised by his mother and his maternal grandparents. Sadly, I never met my father's mother, my grandmother, because she died before my siblings and I were born. My father told us she had been murdered by her boyfriend, which had been extremely challenging for him as a child. With no mother and an absentee father, my father felt responsible for taking care of his two younger sisters. In the thick of World War II, my father joined the US Navy because he knew it would probably be the best way to earn a regular paycheck in order to help out his grandparents.

When I was a child, my father was a huge baseball fan. He was so engulfed with the game that he had Satchel Paige pictures posted throughout the house. I felt like this baseball player from the Negro League was a family member. In fact, my father was so captivated by the game of baseball that he named his first two sons after two of his other favorite baseball players - the oldest son was named Ted after Ted William and his second son was named Robin after Robin Roberts. I believe my father had a secret dream of becoming a professional baseball player himself, but the game of life had other plans for him.

My siblings and I are each about a year apart. My oldest sister is a reincarnation of my maternal grandmother, who was strong and secure within herself. My sister was extroverted and extremely popular by the time we finished grade school. I stayed close to home, watching my mom and mimicking her every move. My mom was shy and introverted, and it was obvious that I took after her. Nonetheless, our parents were very proud of their two oldest little girls - their bookends, as they called us - and they took great pride in all our other siblings as well.

Chapter 2

FAMILY TIES

Our family lived in the village of Cartersville located on the James River, halfway between Richmond and Charlottesville. Established in 1720, Cartersville was full of history and, for the most part, friendly people. However, there was and still is a definite racial divide between the black and white communities. As a young girl I recall using the back door to enter a restaurant and being served just "take-out" because we couldn't sit and eat in there; also seeing the "whites only" and "blacks only" signs above the water fountains and at bathroom facilities. Although the facts have never been personally provided to me, I assume that less than one hundred years prior to my birth, several of my ancestors were celebrating their freedom from slavery in Cartersville, Virginia.

When I was a child, I was told that slaves had been sold along the division line that later separated my black ancestors from the former white slave masters and plantation owners. While slaveholders asserted that their workforce was loyal, they also lived in constant fear of a revolt. White southerners restricted the movement of enslaved African Americans, prevented them from meeting in groups, publicly punished those who attempted to escape slavery, and prohibited them from learning to read. *Could these restrictions be the root of my fears, inherited from my ancestors who were enslaved more than a century prior to my birth?*

The land that our family's house was built on came from my mother's father. His immediate family owned 40 acres of land which he and his brothers shared. Before my grandfather died he gave a share of the land to my mother, who divided it and passed it on to me, my sisters, and brothers. My mom gave me 3 1/2 acres of land, which I still own; and I hope to, one day, build my dream house there.

The land is beautiful, so people are always trying to buy it from me, and I continue to say, "No, it's not for sale." I have so many fond memories of home and, besides that, it's becoming quite valuable. My brother and nephew still live in my family's second Cartersville home. It is actually the house that my father built in the early seventies with the assistance of a contractor. By that time, I had left town with my daughter to live with my grandmother in Pennsylvania. The home that I grew up in was right next door, but it has since fallen down and is now a landfill.

I've always been nostalgic about my hometown. I feel like I'm missing something from there, probably because I left at such a young age. I guess I can say that, ultimately, my goal upon retirement is to return home to Cartersville. Even though I raised my children in New Jersey, I have always considered Cartersville as my home. No matter where I live, as long as I am healthy enough, I want to continue to do what I do now - to give back to the community and empower people through wellness.

My sisters and most of my family continue living in Cartersville and I visit for holidays and other special events. My sisters don't feel nostalgic the way that I do about our hometown, but I feel like a piece of my heart is still there and I haven't been able to put that feeling to rest. Despite the normal ups-and-downs, we were always a close-knit family.

All the black people living in Cartersville are in some way either closely or distantly related to each other. When I was growing up, almost everyone there was a sister, brother, cousin, aunt, uncle, niece, nephew, parent or grandparent to one another. In fact, it was very difficult to find someone who was not related. I guess that's where the expression "kissing cousins" came from - in small towns like mine.

As I reflect, our entire community was mostly family, which was not a good thing due to the fact that there were no clear boundaries on who had sex with whom. We were so naïve that the world of dating your cousin was a normal thing because there were no other black people living in or near our little community. I remember when I was around thirteen-years-old, I met a boy that I really liked a lot and he turned out to be my cousin. What a disappointment that was.

While growing up, the children in our family didn't have many responsibilities. My parents weren't very strict. In fact, they were really quite laid-back. We weren't required to do much work, so we had a lot of play time. My friends and I would often play hide and seek - that was my favorite game. Another favorite pastime was bicycling, even though my six siblings and I only had one bike that we shared amongst us.

Christmas was the overall best time! Each one of us would get one gift and we would also get a brown paper bag filled with an apple and some candy. Plus, we stayed warm and toasty all night long. We had only one heater in the house. It was a wood stove made of cast iron. When my father lit a fire in the wood stove, the heat from the fire would warm the stove and the air in the room. Then, the smoke from the fire was drawn out of the house through the stove's chimney. Normally, the heater was not left burning while we slept.

By 11 P.M. when the fire burned out, we would have to put on our coats to stay warm until around 6 A.M. when my father got up and restarted the fire. But, to make our holiday extra special, my father would keep the house warm on Christmas eve and have the fire going all night, right up until Christmas morning when we were ready to get up.

My father was a great provider, so we were never hungry. We ate beans and biscuits a lot, but we were always satisfied and content. Once a week, my father would give each of us a dime, so we went to the candy store and got lots of candy. We always had a family car for transportation. I remember my father selling moonshine to help make ends meet and to keep us living comfortably.

Mom was a housewife. She didn't work outside of our home until my youngest brother was about twelve years old. When I was separated from my first husband, I did a little housekeeping work in a neighboring community until I left town to live with my grandmother in Pennsylvania.

Back then, life was something surreal, simple and easy. In fact it was so simple that our family didn't even have indoor plumbing. That was not a luxury many of the people in our community were afforded. As long as I can remember, it was certainly not a consideration because everyone had to use an outhouse to go to the bathroom. The outhouse was a small wooden structure that contained a deep hole and a makeshift toilet seat. My father had built it a short distance from the house for quick access. It had no plumbing or sewerage and was extremely unpleasant to use, as well as scary because of the snakes, flies and other insects that you might encounter in and around the structure.

My father later had a new house built with indoor plumbing; but I never got to enjoy it because it was completed shortly after I moved away from home.

Chapter 3

MY MOTHER'S DAUGHTER

When we were young in first grade through sixth grade, my siblings and I walked to my school, which was a two-room schoolhouse located in walking distance from home. When the two-room schoolhouse closed, I changed schools and was bussed to a neighboring community.

I attended the Luther Porter Jackson Intermediate School for three years up until my promotion to the 9th grade, then I met my ex-husband. Our relationship didn't last but a minute, but within that time frame, we conceived my first-born - a baby girl. We got married, and then soon after, we divorced.

My parents were not well-educated. My father just had a third-grade education. He had to work from the time he was a little boy to help feed his family. My mother only completed the eighth grade, but she was very smart, especially in math.

I was the second oldest child in our family. My older sister was the special one. She was very pretty with lots of confidence and she also had lots of friends. I always felt she was loved more by our parents. I was the quiet one and very shy around other people, just like my mother. I strongly believe that my insecurities may have derived from my mother and the way she lacked self-assurance.

Like my mother, I always felt fear around people and instead of shining, I would hide. I know now that every little girl should shine, but I never really loved myself or felt confident about what I could accomplish in life. I remember in school when the teacher looked around the room for students to participate in her lessons, my heart would pound and I would think, *please don't call me!* I would put my head down so the teacher couldn't make eye contact with me, even if I knew the answers. During gym class, I always hid myself in the back of the class behind the taller children and prayed not to be called on to complete an exercise outside of the group.

I was never popular in my class. I attended a school where there was blatant discrimination amongst the light and dark-skinned students. I went to an all-black school. There were no white students in the mix, so the division between the two groups of black students was obvious. My group consisted of the darker-skinned students, who were always called names by the lighter-skinned students who thought they were superior to us. All this discrimination was seen and felt through a child's eyes; thus I became very self-conscious, insecure, and grew up lacking confidence in myself.

I recall one positive experience that occurred when I was in the sixth grade. One of the graduates from my former two-room schoolhouse came back to Cumberland County to speak with the students. I remembered who the graduate was, but I did not think she would recognize me from the elementary school we had attended several years prior. But she did! She actually called out my name, "Barbara," in front of the entire class. I felt so special that my light shined at that moment. For once, probably the first time in my life, I became popular within my group of friends at school because someone with status had remembered my name.

My thoughts and feelings kept me constantly questioning myself, driving me further back inside my shell. I kept wondering, *why was I dark-skinned? Why was I not popular? Why am I so afraid of everything and everyone? Why do I think I will say the wrong thing? Why was I so self-conscious? Why did I lack confidence?*

From GED to Ph.D.

Chapter 4

MOTIVATED BY FEAR

While becoming a teenager, I made all the wrong choices early in life due to a need to be protected and a longing to be loved. At thirteen, my world opened up when I met a guy who was nineteen. Yes, he was older and very experienced, but he told me that he loved me, and I believed him. I began to replace my fear with his love. I should have listened when my mother told me, "Don't go out and play house."

All of a sudden, I felt fearless and loved, so I made bad decisions. Based on my insecurities and lack of life experiences, I discovered that I had become pregnant with my first intercourse. Soon after my discovery, the "love of my life" was taken away to jail for theft, so he didn't even know I was pregnant until he came home six months later. By that time, I was three months short of my delivery.

I turned fourteen with a new baby and was hoping to return to school in the fall. I had completed the ninth grade and was preparing to enter the tenth grade. Then, to my dismay, I was told that I could not return to school unless I was married because, according to school regulation, this was not a good image for the school nor for the other students. Unbeknownst to me, these regulations had been put into place years earlier by a special jurisdiction from the school board.

When my baby's father came home from jail, he asked me to marry him. This was great! I was ecstatic! I was in love, at least what I thought was love. I would be able to return to high school. My plans could finally fall into place and I was very excited. Yes, I would be going back to school as a married woman - or as a child who was trying to be a woman.

So, we were married, and it was a fabulous wedding - one of the happiest days of my life. I wore a borrowed white gown from my now husband's sister, who had gotten married a few months prior. I even borrowed her bridesmaids' dresses for my sisters and friends to wear. I was a beautiful bride! That was one of the best days of my young life. *But what did I really know then about happiness?*

On my wedding day, I felt beautiful and loved and I felt very fortunate. I was truly excited and had no fear about what my future would become because now I finally had someone special, a husband, to always love, cherish, and protect me. However, this did not work out as I had dreamed it would. This man, whom I called "husband", was controlling and abusive.

He took my virginity and held my soul captive with promises and fear. I could not go out the door without being threatened by him. His words still haunt me to this day, "I am going to kill you!" I was still a child living an adult life; but now, with a different kind of fear because I was his wife - his property, as he would constantly remind me - and I feared for my life.

Despite my fears, I continued looking forward to returning to high school, but, unfortunately, that never worked out. My husband owned me, as he stated, and furthering my education was not a part of his agenda. I felt so betrayed by this man after realizing that he only wanted to control me. I was a child with a baby, and he was an older guy who thought I was his sole property.

During the marriage to my first husband, he was physically and mentally abusive. He would hit me just on general principle, but I stayed with him because I thought this was how love was supposed to be. I remember one day; his beating was so severe that I lost my second child that I was pregnant with by him. That was through the grace of God because I certainly did not need a second child at that time. The abuse never stopped, and I wondered, *How did I get myself into this situation?*

What I know for sure is that I was a child trying to live my life as an adult with a child. I was very confused and did not know the next step of my life. I experienced lots of fear and anxiety. My mother and father were very supportive of me and my baby girl. They were the perfect grandparents. Regina was their first grandchild and they loved her as if she was their own child.

To be pregnant at a young age seemed to be a normal thing within our community. My mother was just sixteen when her first child was born; but, unlike my ex-husband, her husband - my dad - was kind, caring, and never abusive. The man I married had become my new parent with husband privileges and I had become a wife and mother living in poverty off of minimum funds a week for food and other essentials.

I wasn't married yet when my daughter was born, but when I got married, the three of us – my daughter, my husband Walter, and I - lived with my parents. We stayed with them for almost the entire first year of our marriage and then my husband got fed up with the living arrangement. Eventually, he told me that we would have to move to his mother's home. That was so difficult for me. Walter was twenty-one, but I was just a fifteen-year-old child who had suddenly become a wife and a parent, having to leave the comfort of my parents' house for the first time in my life to begin a confused and uncertain existence at my in-laws' home.

One day, just before we moved from my parents' house, Walter and I were sitting in a car and he had another woman in the back seat of the car with us. Unbeknownst to me, she was actually the person he was having an affair with, but I didn't realize it because I was so naïve to this man and blinded by what I called love. All of a sudden, my husband hit me in front of this woman and I humbled myself to him and took his abuse right in front of her.

At that point, I was so depressed that I became suicidal. I wanted to kill myself, so I took a bottle of Tylenol. Fortunately, my sister got to me in time. She made me drink something which forced me to throw up and she kept me walking and talking until I got stronger. I just wanted to die because I didn't want to leave my mother's home, but I had to go with him. After all, he was my husband. But the intimate partner abuse soon forced me to go to live with my grandmother in Harrisburg, Pennsylvania.

My mother-in-law was very kind to me and her granddaughter. She knew how abusive her son was, so she cared for us and protected us as much as possible. When my husband told me I couldn't go to church anymore, my mother-in-law told him, "No, she is going to church!" She always tried to take care of me so I wouldn't get hurt in the process. Even after her son and I got divorced, my mother-in-law and I stayed in close touch with each other right up until the day she died.

Walter was so bold that he would come to my parents' home while I was visiting them and hit me without a second thought. As time went on, I got out of that bad situation. After a tumultuous two years of marriage, my father helped me to escape from my abusive husband. Finally, at the age of seventeen, I was able to leave Walter and move out of my small community to start a new journey with my daughter, who was then just three years old.

The day Regina was born had been the happiest day of my life and, during that dreadful time in my life, she was my only reason to go on living. I was not sure what I knew about being a mother at that age, but at least I knew she was mine to love and cherish. My baby daughter's birth had truly been one of my biggest blessings.

Little did I know that three years later, I would meet the greatest love of my life and I would finally experience a series of happy days. I was still a teenager, barely 18-years-old. As time went on, I got out of a bad situation. After an abusive and tumultuous marriage, my daughter and I moved away from my parents' home and went to Harrisburg, Pennsylvania to live with my grandmother.

PART TWO

From GED to Ph.D.

Chapter 5

DISCOVERING
MY SOUL MATE

S hortly after I moved to Pennsylvania, my daughter and I moved to Long Island to live with my aunt. My sister, Cally, moved there a few months later.

I knew who Spencer was because when we were children we lived in the same town. I didn't really know him well, though. I knew his mother and father and I went to school with his younger sister and brothers. He was a few years older than me. I was friendly with Spencer's siblings, but he had joined the military, then he went out of town to college, and after that, he lived in New Jersey and worked at CBS Television Network in New York City.

While I was still living with my parents, Spencer would come home to visit his family in Cartersville during his military breaks. I was visiting his sister one day when he came home on furlough. I would sometimes encounter him at his mother's house, and we would talk, but it had been just a casual friendship - nothing special.

While living in Long Island, I was reacquainted with Spencer, but by now, I had been unhappily married and I was single again. Spencer's cousin, who lived nearby, was coincidently dating my sister. I became better acquainted with Spencer when his cousin brought him to my aunt's house to hang out with my sister and me. Our relationship soon became serious.

I began to date Spencer, whom I soon realized was my soulmate sent from God. Spencer made me feel safe and he respected me. He became both my protector and mentor. Perhaps at the time, he was another father image to me because, after all, he was several years older than me. Whatever the reason, it didn't matter because it was obviously going to be the perfect union. I kept asking myself though, *Did God send this man into my life to journey with me through my fears?* Lord knows I still had lots of fears. This man accepted me and my sweet little daughter and then, together, we became the proud parents of two additional children, our wonderful sons.

When Spencer and I got together seriously as a couple, I had one child, Regina, who was four. I loved raising my daughter and Spencer really loved the fact that I had a little girl. He accepted her as his own child and made sure she had everything she wanted and needed. He really spoiled her.

Regina helped Spencer to heal after his own daughter was killed in a car accident. She had been around the same age as Regina when the tragedy occurred. Ironically, Regina's father died around the same time. I told Spencer, "You know what? God gave Regina a father and He gave you a daughter." One day, Regina said excitedly, "Mommy, *he* said I could call him Daddy." From that day on, she started calling Spencer "Daddy." It was a heart-warming realization.

Chapter 6

THE FUTURE IS NOW

Spencer and I established a loving relationship. The three of us became a happy family and took our first step toward declaring the seriousness of our union by moving in together. I was nineteen years old when we relocated to Paterson, New Jersey. Soon after, we purchased our first home, because our family was growing. We had two sons and a daughter. We were a picture-perfect family and I was excited.

I was 22 years old when I married Spencer. He presented me with a whole new lifestyle. Spencer was a news director for CBS Network news. He introduced me to the people at his job, but I had a difficult time with meeting new acquaintances. Because I wasn't very well-educated, I felt insecure around them. At the time, I was so shy and intimidated that I feared having a conversation with Spencer's co-workers because I thought my words would come out wrong and I didn't want to embarrass him or myself. Spencer took my feelings to heart and gave it some serious thought. He wanted me to find my own path and encouraged me to think seriously about my future.

I wasn't really sure what I wanted to do at the time. I just knew that I wanted to do something relevant. I could just feel it within my spirit, but I only had a ninth-grade education, and I had no idea how to move forward. I was stuck.

One day, Spencer took my hand and said, "Barbara, why don't you go back to school and get an education? That would be a good place to start." So, after mulling it over, I took Spencer's advice and began the process. I went to a community college and registered to take classes toward earning my General Educational Equivalent Diploma (GED). Now that I was in pursuit of a specific goal, I challenged myself and everything began to evolve for me. That didn't work out right away because I had absolutely no confidence in myself. I was afraid of failing and thus, I became very negative.

I knew I was protected and loved, but this fear monster that I carried around inside of me still existed. Even though I had this wonderful family, the feeling of unworthiness and the lack of confidence still presented itself on occasions when I was confronted by people who were highly educated and well-versed. This, I realized, was a fear of never having a sense of importance or pride. I was consumed with fear and had no confidence to start my new journey to further my education. Here I was, 25-years-old, returning to school after dropping out of high school ten years prior. I did not know how to read well, certain words were foreign to me, and pronunciation was always a struggle. However, at Spencer's suggestion, my journey started with acquiring my GED, which proved to be a very difficult task for me.

I began attending a community college to earn twenty-four credits that would give me a GED, but fear stopped my progression. I became negative, overwhelmed, and full of anxiety, so I dropped out of the program at the community college.

Chapter 7

I'M COMING OUT!

S pencer was determined to erase all my doubts, fears, and insecurities. Once he made up his mind that this was what I needed to do, he wouldn't let me talk myself out of it or quit. He insisted that I re-enlist in the GED class. I took his advice and instead of going to the community college, I went to the local high school to register. That worked out better. I felt more comfortable with the other students in attendance because they were closer to my age and skillset, and the teachers were more patient.

GED stands for general educational equivalent diploma. GED also refers to the certificate that you earn by passing certain tests. The GED certificate proved that I had educational skills that are similar to those of a high school graduate. To qualify, I had to be tested in four subjects, none of which I had any knowledge: Math, Science, Social Studies, and Reasoning through Language Arts (RLA). Spencer continued to encourage me and he also found a tutor for me.

Then, my loving husband Spencer, the father of my three children who loved me more than I loved myself, said, "Go back and take the test." I got myself up one morning and went to the high school where the GED test was being offered. Still very fearful and apprehensive, I prayed before I took the test, completed all the questions, and left with high anxiety.

It took several weeks to get the results from my GED test, but when I received that diploma in the mail, my life changed. I was so excited! I had passed the test! More than ten years after I had dropped out of high school, I was finally a high school graduate.

I had studied hard and earned my GED in 1980. After I got my GED, Spencer was right there to encourage me, once again, to take the next step toward a better future. He asked me, "What are you going to do now, Barbara?"

I told him that I didn't know, but I was beginning to feel free of the invisible shackles that had been holding me down. I was exhilarated and probably felt like Diana Ross did when she made the shocking decision to break free and leave her record label. In fact, I walked around singing one of Diana's signature hits, "I'm Coming Out," which expressed her declaration of independence as a singer, and mine as a high school graduate. I was extremely excited to have my GED and I wanted the world to know. That was a really good feeling. I was so proud of myself and I was finally ready to come out of my shell - or so I thought.

I had so much - a loving husband, a wonderful family – but still I felt very insecure within myself. *Why did I continue to question my successes and why did I continue to deal with my fears? Could my ancestors really have something to do with my uncertain journey?*

Now, I will attempt to shed some light on my life as a wife and mother of three children and the journey that has made me an *EXCEPTIONAL WOMAN!*

From GED to Ph.D.

Chapter 8

JUST BELIEVE

I do believe that many of my insecurities began to surface when I started being bussed to the new public school in Cumberland County. I was just nine years old then and had to leave the safety net of our two-room schoolhouse and the closeness of community friends in order to be exposed to something bigger. My longtime friends and I intermingled with the black kids from neighboring communities, but even though we all were black, we suffered from the same type of discrimination that we expected to experience from white kids. We were teased, heckled, and talked about, mainly because we came from the "other side of the tracks."

Here I was at a new crossroad at the age of twenty-two. I had earned my GED, yet my old insecurities were still coming back. They continued to haunt me even as I prepared to enter college. This time, though, I forced myself to move forward instead of giving up and dropping out. I knew I wanted to do something important for me, for my future, and for my husband. I also wanted to set an example for my three children, so I decided to enroll in college. But then, after thinking about it, I told Spencer, "I can't do that." And he said, "Yes, you can!" So I believed him and then I repeated, "Yes, I can!"

Imagine that! Me, the teenage mother, the high school dropout, the person who could barely read or comprehend what she did read! I was planning to enroll in college!

As I recall, my higher educational journey actually started when I found a book by Norman Vincent Peale, which my husband had stored in the attic. It was "The Power of Positive Thinking." I read that book from cover to cover, cut out passages and taped them all over my space. I even took one passage to bed with me: "I can do all things through Christ, who strengthens me."

I still wondered, *How was I going to be successful in college and what will I major in once I get into college? Would the admissions department accept me without SAT scores? How was this going to happen for me?* Spencer's words were, "You can do this, Barbara!" So I completed the application for enrollment into college and I was accepted. Wow! God was still working for me.

Chapter 9

I WAS THE EXCEPTION

After Spencer and I did some research, we decided on what turned out to be the perfect choice for furthering my education. That's when I enrolled in William Paterson University's nursing program.

William Paterson University is among the largest universities in the state of New Jersey, with nearly 10,000 students and approximately 82,000 living alumni, including almost 65,000 alumni in New Jersey.

Known for excellence in nursing education, William Paterson University's nursing program prepares students for entry level practice as professional nurses in a variety of settings, including hospitals, clinics, and community health organizations. Graduates are well-prepared for the National Council Licensure Examination (NCLEX), administered by the New Jersey Board of Nursing, to become professional nurses. They also gain a strong foundation for advanced education at the master's and doctoral levels.

There was no waiting list. I got the acceptance letter almost immediately to enter the nursing program. But why was this? When I spoke with the registrar's office, they informed me that there was a waiting list for the nursing program. Yet, I was just accepted without waiting for anything! *Was this God's divine guidance for me? Was this my purpose?*

My fear had become ten times higher. I was not feeling as worthy as the other students. Plus, most of the other students were directly out of high school. I thought, *they must know more than I do.* I came from a small town, an all-black community in the country. How in the world was I supposed to compete with these intelligent, young, diverse students?

Despite all my insecurities, I started college in the fall of 1981 at twenty-eight years old. After I completed all my prerequisites for a major, I still wondered, *what will that major be?* Spencer had planted the idea in my head to pursue nursing as a career. A nursing career had never occurred to me. I certainly had no nurses in my family, and I did not know any nurses personally; but Spencer enthusiastically said to me, "You should become a nurse!" I knew that I cared about people and I was compassionate - he also knew that about me. Again I wondered, *was Spencer sent from God? How did he figure that out?* I was not sure if a nursing career was what I wanted to pursue, but there were no other dreams or ideas in my head. I then enrolled in the William Paterson College (which is now William Paterson University) Nursing program to pursue what would become my life's passion.

I had to take several prerequisites before declaring a major. I gasped when I learned that one of the required courses was algebra, which was Greek to me. I had never studied this type of math in my life and asked myself, *how do I conquer this algebra?* For the life of me, I couldn't understand why algebra was a prerequisite to higher learning. But after researching it, I realized that I couldn't go very far without the fundamentals of algebra and understood that I couldn't afford to exclude it from my curriculum. To make matters worse, my professor said to me, "You have *never* had algebra before?" emphasizing *never* under his breath. I then became fearful and began to question myself. *How is this going to happen? Am I setting myself up for failure?* Then, I remembered the tutoring that my God-sent husband had offered to pay for. This wonderful man that I married paid for further tutoring in order to assure my success and it worked. Lord, I do not know how, but I did it!

I persevered, managed to master algebra, and earned a passing grade. This was another milestone in my life where I realized, once again, that I can do all things through Christ, who strengthens me.

I had taken Spencer's advice, stepped up to the plate, and embarked upon my nursing career. Having been accepted in nursing school, I enthusiastically started my journey in Nursing 101. I was on top of the world. As I progressed, I took English, Philosophy, and all the other prerequisite courses that were required to enter the field of Nursing.

Within those prerequisite courses, I had my first lab and needed to be paired up with a partner. I was the exception in my classes as the oldest student and also because I was married with three young children to care for. The Lab skills class was fun, but I had lots of anxiety. I was in my glory, though, a little intimidated and shy around people, but I did the necessary work. When it came to the skills exam, I lightheartedly said to my instructor, "My life is your hands."

She told me, "I will not accept that statement. It's on you!" I didn't know how to respond to that, so I shied away, and fear started to attack my soul. I was so nervous. My hands became sweaty, and my heart was beating fast. I wondered, *How do I stop this?* When it was time for the exam, I said a prayer to calm myself down, organized my thoughts, and passed the Skills Course 101. Several students did not make it through, but I did. I had crossed over to the next level and was very proud and excited, although I still had difficulty with the pronunciations of some of the medical words.

My clinic instructor said, "Barbara, if you don't learn to pronounce the words, you will have problems moving ahead." This was so true. The lack of pronunciation impacted my confidence and escalated my fear as I journeyed through nursing school while dealing with other professionals. I practiced the words over and over again, but I was still not sure if my pronunciation was correct. My immature thoughts arose. *Am I saying the words incorrectly? Are they laughing at me? What is wrong with me?* All of those negative thoughts were on my mind, so I prayed about it and gradually replaced them with positive thoughts like *Look at me now and how far I have come!*

With all my education, fear would constantly remain with me, but I did not allow that green-eyed monster to stop me from accomplishing what God had planted in my soul. Throughout my educational journey, I would still have problems with my vocabulary; but I knew I was not the smartest student in my classes, so I read and reread everything until I understood what was required of me to become successful. I am not sure if I needed to prove something to others or just to myself, but I did whatever I had to do to succeed with my goals.

Still, I kept wondering, *why was this success not enough for me to walk outside of my fears?* All I knew was that everywhere I went, Mr. Fear followed me. *How was I to overcome this monster and start living the life that was promised to me?*

Chapter 10

GRADUATION DAY

I knew that earning my Bachelor of Science degree wouldn't be easy, but Spencer lit a fire under me, and I was determined to make him proud. At that time, we had three children. Spencer and I had two boys from our union, plus our daughter, Regina.

When I first went to college, I didn't know what I wanted to study and Spencer suggested that I should be a nurse, but I told him that I didn't want to be a nurse because I didn't know anything about that field. Spencer knew that I wasn't sure what career to pursue so he planted that in my brain, and I pushed forward to complete my next goal.

One of the things I had to do to get passing grades in my math class was to study algebra at least two to four hours every day. Because I had absolutely no understanding of algebra, I needed a lot of tutoring to help me get through that class, but I did it and I passed the course. I went to school during the day and Spencer worked nights. He was home from his job at CBS News by 10:00 AM. That worked out well because I was able to attend classes and he would be available for the children, especially when there were school meetings or events.

Fear was always present for me, though. I couldn't stop thinking that the other students were better than me and knew more than I did. I remember taking a class with over one hundred other students who were pre-nursing, pre-med and all the other science majors. One day, my professor announced that the lowest grade she gave someone was a zero, but she said that she would give points to that student for their name only. I knew she was referring to my paper, because I did not understand anything at all about the subject, which was Microbiology. *Yes, I was the student with that famous F!*

At that instant, I became so sad and depressed. I felt like the world was coming to an end and I was a failure! I wondered, *what do I do now? Do I continue or do I drop out?* All the negative thoughts that I had were causing me to go crazy. I experienced so much fear and became tremendously overwhelmed by a huge lack of confidence. As usual, Spencer encouraged me. I ended up receiving tutoring for the course, took control of the subject matter, and read the text book over and over until I comprehended the concept and passed the class, which brought my thinking to another level. Even my professor was impressed with my success.

Despite my despair and all the hurdles I encountered, I continued to pass all the science classes that I needed in order to enter the nursing program, with the exception of a pre-summer course, which I, unfortunately, failed. I had an extremely busy schedule then and there had been no time for tutoring because this was a fast-paced course. It was another crushing devastation to my soul. That's when one of my insensitive professors told me, "Barbara, you should quit, because the field of nursing is not for you."

It seems like yesterday when that professor was discussing gluconeogenesis. She drew a diagram on the board to demonstrate a model of the concept, and then without further explanation, that topic was presented on an exam. I drew the diagram replication as it was given in class. However, she did not want a replication, but rather an intensive description of the understanding of the process, which I didn't have, primarily because I was afraid to ask the essential questions to understand the concept.

After the professor told me, "I do not think you are a candidate for college," I came home and cried like a baby. Spencer said, "You go back and retake that course." I was very hesitant about retaking the course. I wanted to give up, but my husband would not allow me to quit. Again, I got tutored, but I learned something from the past. I realized that I could not rush learning because it is a process, not just a summer course for me. With silent prayers every second, I retook the course with the same professor and earned an A.

While thinking back about my professors, someone special still stands out in my mind. I had a very caring professor who taught my philosophy class and he came to my rescue in the beginning of my course. Philosophy was required for my degree, but I didn't understand anything about it. At the end of my course, my professor said to me, "You know, Barbara, I'm going to pass you because I've seen the determination in you, and I see that you can do more. Don't get me wrong, you deserve an "F," but I'm going to give you a passing grade because you only need to *pass* the course." I was so grateful that all I could do was cry. And with my professor's ongoing encouragement, I kept learning how to organize my thoughts and I finally understood how to study.

My nursing class started out with one hundred and sixty students. With each semester, students were weened out and it became a blessing every year for me to continue. I should have been excited, even if it was only for the moment, but it had been such a challenging journey and I was both exhausted and exhilarated at the same time. Out of the one hundred and sixty students that started out, only sixty graduated. Fewer than half the students had the privilege to walk and I was one of those graduates. I was the oldest and the only black graduate, with two Hispanic students, and the other fifty-seven graduates were Caucasian. Despite all my fears, I made it through!

I completed the required courses and earned my Bachelor of Science in Nursing from William Paterson College. I was extremely gratified to get all my credits approved for this great moment. Finally, after a six-year process, it was graduation day, May 17, 1987. I wore my black and orange regalia and, at the age of thirty-four, I walked. What a glorious day it was for me!

Chapter 11

CONNECTING THE DOTS

My professional life started soon after I received my Bachelor of Science in Nursing (BSN) degree. The next step was acquiring a license to practice. I was so grateful to be at this point in my life. *Had I conquered my fears? The feeling of not being important or the feeling of being less than I was?* The degree should have been proof to others that I was worthy, but I was still not sure. This should have been my day of "I can do all things through Christ," but something was still missing.

Despite my recent accomplishment, I continued to feel inferior to others and my fears persisted. Then I took the exam for my license and failed. I went into a depression, which increased my low self-esteem and impacted my deep fears. My hero of a husband began with his words of encouragement, "You worked so hard. How are you going to let an exam throw you off your game?" I began to listen to Spencer and asked him what I could do to pass the exam. He told me, "Study for it, put your time and effort into it, and retake it!" I did all of that, went back to take the exam, and passed it. I became a Registered Nurse with a Bachelor of Science degree! I was so excited. I had no fears at that time - only joy and optimism.

Everything worked out. Again, I overcame my fears while Spencer enjoyed spending time with our children. Plus, the neighbors' children would always come to our house to hang out with our children and they were always welcomed with open arms. It was one big happy family then and, to this day, they still call me "Mom." That's the way I grew up, though. All the neighborhood kids would gather at our house because my mom loved to have us and our friends around her.

I often think of the sacrifices Spencer and I had to make, and I regret the time I missed with my children when they were growing up. My children and their friends will always remember me sitting at the desk in my den, studying day and night. During those years, I had very little time for them. They spent more time with their father than with me.

I was still trying to fulfill my life's purpose, but I started my new journey with so much fear and trepidation. After earning my Bachelor of Science Degree in Nursing, I began working at a big medical center as a nurse. However, my fear was so intense that I quit my job within two weeks. Then with much remorse, I wondered, *What do I do now? How do I take this RN license to a place where God has a purpose for me? A place where my fears will be decreased and allow me to function?*

Soon after, I ended up landing a position at a small community hospital, which was perfect. It enabled me to gain some confidence, especially because I was finally caring for patients. This was when I knew that God had a purpose for me. As I met each new patient, I was still experiencing insecurities and fear, but I was surviving as an RN. I worked at that small hospital for two years. Then, through the grace of God, I landed a position at the Veterans Hospital in East Orange, New Jersey as a staff nurse. I still had fears, but I believed I could endure because I was following my purpose.

Finally, my path was becoming clear. My confidence was growing, my passion for nursing had evolved, and my journey to obtain a higher education escalated. First, I took a new position as a Case Manager within the Veterans Hospital. Then, because my job consisted of building a closer relationship with the doctors for the benefit of the patients, my fear crept in again. However, I prayed fervently as I journeyed along, "I can do all things through Christ who strengthens me."

From GED to Ph.D.

Chapter 12

MY MASTER
OF SCIENCE DEGREE

I worked at the Veterans Hospital as a staff nurse and Case Manager. While working there full-time, I embarked upon another educational journey. In 2001, I decided to return to school to complete my Master of Science degree as a nurse practitioner. I enrolled in Saint Peter's College in Englewood Cliffs, New Jersey.

I am not sure how it happened, but I did not fail any courses at Saint Peter's College. In fact, I completed my master's degree in two and a half years and graduated Cum Laude with a 3.50 GPA. I was actually an honor student! How great was that! My accomplishments had exceeded my expectations. This was because God had an even greater purpose for me. Even with my fears, Gods carried me through with high honors.

I remember taking a pharmacy class, which was a very intense course with lots of information needed to succeed. In my class, there was another black student, who did not pair up with me because she felt that I was not smart enough. It so happened that all her friends were Caucasian, but when she discovered I was earning an "A" in the class, she suddenly became my "best friend." To this day, ironically, we have maintained our friendship. Just a little thought for your mind, *you should not judge a person by what you think that person may or may not know.*

While I continued to work at the Veterans Hospital, I became a nurse practitioner with a certification in Oncology, running my own clinic in Medical Oncology. I was extremely excited. This certification was very difficult, but I passed it.

What an accomplishment I had under my belt! I should have been overjoyed. My patients and their families respected me and depended on me for their loved ones' care, but I couldn't stop wondering, *Why did I still have these feelings of fear and why was I feeling like I was less than others? Will I have these negative feelings for life or is it possible to be myself without fear? Will it ever be possible for me to walk with the confidence I need to become my true self?*

I was still journeying, trying to prove to myself and others that I am somebody. Then, I remembered Martin Luther King Jr's speech on your "Life Blueprint." Number one in your life blueprint is "A deep belief in your dignity and worth, your 'somebodiness.' Have the firm conviction that life has ultimate significance and that you are here for a purpose."

Was this me? I had no belief in my self-worth and no blueprint for my life. Is this the reason I have no inner peace within myself or is this the genetic make-up of my destiny?

I persevered and kept moving forward. As I traveled through my educational journey, my thoughts were always, *how did I get here with all my limitations? God must truly have a purpose for me.* I took all the prerequisites. I even took general science and biochemistry and passed on the first try. I was so proud of myself, but I still felt I needed to prove myself to others and that I was just as smart as they were. Yet, what I did not realize was that I didn't require anyone's approval - only my own. I did not realize that during the time I was discovering myself, God was always placing good people in my life to direct my path for His purpose and mine.

From GED to Ph.D.

Chapter 13

THE *EXTRAORDINARY*
BARBARA V. CRUMP

I continued to journey through my work at the Veteran's Hospital and my educational aspirations. While I searched online and thought about the possibility of pursuing another degree, The University of Phoenix picked up my search and enrolled me in their Ph.D. program.

The flexibility of virtual learning fit well with my lifestyle at that time. I had one-on-one connections with experienced faculty and collaborative opportunities with my classmates. I also had the freedom to learn when and where I wanted without the time-consuming commute or semester-long commitment.

When I enrolled in the Ph.D. program, I did not fully understand it. That was me - no blueprint for my life, but there was a greater power directing me, even at the age of 56. In 2010, I entered the Ph.D. program, even though an online education was going be a completely new experience for me.

While pursuing my Ph.D., I encountered an extraordinary oncologist who helped me along my journey. Dr. Chang knew my passions. I was still working at the Veterans Hospital at the time. When I took care of my patients, he saw how passionate and concerned I was about them and he noticed that I never deviated from those traits. I remained steadfast in my actions and upheld my mindset because I believed that everyone should be treated with respect when they were patients in the hospital, especially when they were dying.

Dr. Chang told me, "Come here, Barbara, let me show you something." He led me out of the office, took me to the nursing station in the oncology unit, and walked with me down the hallway. Then he continued, "This man is laying in the hallway dying. This should not be happening. How do we maintain the dignity of this patient?" I responded, "No, he shouldn't be laying here alone, dying." With that example, Dr. Chang steered me toward the right path concerning my dissertation, which was entitled "Exploring Nurses' Perceptions of Dignity During End-of-Life Care."

In preparation for my doctorate dissertation, I interviewed eleven oncology nurses. They wanted curriculums in and required a palliative care course for nurses to explore dignity during the end-of-life. I published and presented my work. I completed my dissertation with Phoenix University online in 2016. My excitement was heightened when I passed my comprehensive exam on the first try. I knew then that I was on my way. It had been a six-year process, but I persevered, and I did it!

My graduation took place in May 2017 at the Verizon Center in Washington, DC. At the age of sixty-five, forty-nine years after becoming a high school dropout, I had become an honor student. What an achievement in my life! Having earned my Doctorate of Philosophy in Nursing, I am proud to introduce myself as the *extraordinary* Barbara V. Crump, PhD, RN, NP-C, AOCNP.

Yet still, I have no peace.

Chapter 14

MY BLUEPRINT FOR LIFE

After working at the Veterans Hospital for twenty-five years, I retired in order to care for my elderly mother, who was terminally ill with colon cancer. I returned to Cartersville, the little community where I was born, and stayed there and cared for my mother until the end-of her life in March 2017. Regrettably, my mother could not attend my graduation, which occurred two months later.

After my mother passed, I received my first position as an assistant professor of nursing at a university near my home in Teaneck. I thought, *perhaps teaching is my purpose.* And it felt warm and comfortable as I walked onto that campus. I knew this was my destined place, but I was wrong because it was misery. Throughout my stay at that university, I was bullied by the other two professors and the Dean. I was told that I lacked confidence. They did not mentor me; instead, they wanted to see me fail.

Being an educator was a new experience for me. During my first semester, I taught a class called Nursing Foundations.

As a part of the class, the students needed to pass a math test. I was to give them the tools for success and I did that. I had thirty students and they all passed the math exam. The Associate Dean told me, "This is impossible, it has never happened before." She came into the classroom and started to go through the exams while the students were sitting in the classroom. Then she asked me, "How could this be?"

What was she insinuating? After all, I did not develop the exam - it was a university exam. I felt so hurt by her actions. *How could people that should be your colleagues be so disrespectful? How was this possible?* My dignity was destroyed within my own profession. I felt she had stepped on my soul. *Was this really my soul?* That's a place where only God resides, so it must have been my heart because I could not breathe after the visit from the Dean.

I had such a difficult time holding back my tears, even when a student walked into my office. I should have been composed, but my heart was bleeding and I broke down in front of the student. She prayed with me. After two years, I left teaching and went back to my prior position as a nurse practitioner. In dismay, I even dropped the Ph.D. from my title. But then I wondered, *Was this supposed to be a lesson for me to accomplish His plan?*

I realize now that I had to go through that experience to build my strength. I kept thinking about Martin Luther King Jr.'s words, "Don't allow anybody to make you feel that you're nobody."

Always feel that you count. Always feel that you have worth, and always feel that your life has ultimate significance. These words have, indeed, become my blueprint for life.

From GED to Ph.D.

FAMILY SNAPSHOTS

Dear Barbara,

Thank you for your care & concern for my Father during his illness and until you took him to Heaven 9-27.

My Father loved you — and I see why, you were wonderful to him and our family.

We are sad, but have faith that all of you did everything possible to extend his life and keep him comfortable.

Thank you for assisting me through th all.

Tender Thoughts. God BLESS you Barbara!

xo Helena

TECT4409X
©AGC, Inc.

From GED to Ph.D.

Department of Veterans Affairs

Special Contribution Award

Presented to

Barbara V. Crump, RN

*for a unique contribution to the
mission of the Department.*

KENNETH H. MIZRACH, DIRECTOR
VA NJ HEALTH CARE SYSTEM

December 8, 2006

VA FORM 3483b JUL 1992(R)

APPENDIX A: *Certificates, Awards, Letters, Media*

DEPARTMENT OF VETERANS AFFAIRS
New Jersey Health Care System

■ **VA Medical Centers**

East Orange Campus
385 Tremont Avenue
East Orange, NJ 07018
(973) 676-1000

Lyons Campus
151 Knollcroft Road
Lyons, NJ 07939
(908) 647-0180

■ **VA Community Based
Outpatient Clinics
(CBOCs)**

James J. Howard CBOC
970 Route 70
Brick, NJ 08724
(732) 206-8900

Elizabeth CBOC
654 East Jersey Street
Suite 2A
Elizabeth, NJ 07206
(908) 994-0120

Fort Monmouth CBOC
Patterson Army Health Clinic
Building 1075, Stephenson Ave.
Fort Monmouth, NJ 07703
(732) 532-4500

Hackensack CBOC
385 Prospect Avenue
Hackensack, NJ 07601
(201) 487-1390

Jersey City CBOC
115 Christopher Columbus Dr.
Jersey City, NJ 07302
(201) 435-3055

Morristown CBOC
340 West Hanover Ave.
Morristown, NJ 07960
(973) 539-9791

Newark CBOC
20 Washington Place
Newark, NJ 07102
(973) 645-1441

New Brunswick CBOC
317 George Street
New Brunswick, NJ 08901
(732) 729-0646

Paterson CBOC
275 Getty Avenue
Paterson, NJ 07503
(973) 247-1666

Trenton CBOC
171 Jersey Street
Building 36
Trenton, NJ 08611
(609) 989-2355

March 15, 2010

Barbara Crump, NP-C
Department of Veterans Affairs
East Orange Campus
385 Tremont Avenue
East Orange, New Jersey 07018

Dear Ms. Crump:

Congratulations! Based on criteria for the Gold Oak Leaf Awards Program, eight hours of time off are granted to you for achieving a high level of patient satisfaction within the VA New Jersey Health Care System. Patient satisfaction scores were based on the 2009 Survey of Health Care Experiences of Patients (SHEP) for inpatients seen in the Medical Bed Sections at the East Orange Campus.

Results demonstrate that seven Hospital-Consumer Assessment of Hospital Providers and Systems also known as H-CAHPS composites (previously named Veteran Health Service Standards or VHSS) were higher than the VHA national average in the Medical Bed Sections at the East Orange Campus. These standards include Communication with Nurses, Communication with Doctors, Communication about Medication, Nursing Services, Pain Control, Cleanliness, and Quietness.

The time off award must be used by September 15, 2010.

A copy of this letter will be forwarded to Human and Learning Resources Management.

Your effort to enhance patient satisfaction within the VA New Jersey Health Care System is deeply appreciated.

Sincerely,

KENNETH H. MIZRACH
Director

August 8, 2007

Dear Mrs. Crump,
I had the pleasure to meet you yesterday when I drove my parents Richard and Jane Blankley (yes — this really old Dick and Jane.) to The hospital.

On behalf of my parents, my sister Carol and brothers and myself, I want to thank you for your patience and efforts to make a difficult situation less stressful. You're probably thinking, "I'm just doing my job." But we all know that. But we all know many people who do their job and don't do well. You do your job exceedingly well and we are deeply appreciative.

John Marker

Department of Veterans Affairs New Jersey Health Care System

Certificate of Recognition

presented to

Barbara Crump, MSN, RN, ANP

for obtaining the Nurse Practitioner Certification.

On this 11th day of May 2011, we would like to recognize you for being a valued member of Patient Care Services.

Patrick Troy
Associate Director
Patient Care Services

From GED to Ph.D.

'That's my home'

BY EMILY HOLLINGSWORTH
The Farmville Herald

The Farmville Herald

August 1, 2018

Barbara Crump has experienced a lot in the decades she has pursued her education. Yet while moving to another state, working for more than 25 years in nursing and receiving her doctorate in her 60s, she still considers the place she grew up, Ampthill Road in Cartersville, her home.

She said she was 15 when she became pregnant and had to drop out of high school in ninth grade. The pregnancy, societal attitudes at the time, as well as intimate partner abuse, forced her to live with her grandmother and aunt in Harrisburg, Pennsylvania.

"You really couldn't go back to school if you were pregnant and were not married," Crump, 65, said.

She said most of her family continues to live in Cartersville, and she visits for holidays and other events.

Crump, whose maiden name is Johnson, moved to New Jersey in the 1970s.

She returned to school and received her General Educational Development (GED), and in 1987 obtained her bachelor's degree of science in nursing from William Patterson University in Wayne, New Jersey.

She said while she was proud of her education achievements, it was not an easy process.

"As you grow and develop, you get to know yourself," Crump said. "But I didn't have that opportunity to get to know myself because I had a child. I couldn't complete my high school, get to know people, have those friends that you connect with in high school. I didn't have that. So it was all a process for me."

She credits her pursuit for education in part to her current husband, Spencer, who not only encouraged her to return to school, but who also grew up in Cartersville with her family.

Crump, while also raising her children and working full time, pursued and received her Master of Science from Saint Peter's College to become a nurse practitioner in 2003.

She continued to work as an advanced practice nurse and in 2010, began to study for her doctorate of Philosophy in Nursing from Phoenix University.

It was a 6-year process, but she said the late nights and study hours were worth it to pursue a field she was passionate about, and to be an example to her children and 12 grandchildren.

"They're excited," Crump said about her family's response to her receiving her doctorate

Pictured is Barbara Crump, second from right, who received her doctorate during a ceremony in Washington D.C. Pictured are, from left, son Anthony Crump, daughter Regina Crump, husband Spencer Crump I, Barbara and Spencer Crump II.

in 2016. "I'm trying to encourage them and mentor them."

"You just have to do the work," Crump said. "Education is opportunity for everyone. It's out there. You just need to do it to get there, and I tell my grandkids that too. If you do the work, you will get the benefits."

"You have to give up some things, too," Crump said, laughing. "Sometimes you don't sleep because you're studying for exams."

She said her doctorate dissertation was a qualitative study on nurses perception of how patients should be treated at the end of their lives.

Crump said she interviewed 11 oncology nurses for "Exploring nurses' perceptions of dignity during end-of-life care."

"They wanted curriculums in undergrad for palliative care (care for people with terminal illnesses) and maybe a workshop to discuss dignity and reflection on self-dignity, so a lot of

that was in communication, and communication is very important when you're dealing with death and dying," Crump said, noting the importance of having training people to help them at the end of their lives.

"That's my passion. Dignity, respect, and just empowering people in death and dying," Crump said. "We shouldn't suffer. We have hospice, we have that. But it can be a struggle, and how do we make it better?"

She said she is going to continue her research, developing a model for end of life care, and look into ways to implement the model.

She said this issue became particularly relevant when her mother became ill and died in March 2017 of colon cancer.

"I stopped work, I came home when she was dying," Crump said. I took care of her at the hospice, make sure she had good quality, had the family around her. It

is very important."

She said she is now working to create a mentorship program in New Jersey high schools and colleges to help students interested in pursuing nursing.

Ultimately, she said her goal upon retirement is to return to Cartersville.

"That's my home," Crump said. "Even though I raised my children here in New Jersey, I always called it my home." She said she wants to continue to do what she does now, give back to the community and empower people through wellness.

To view the following article "Patient Dignity", go to:

cjon.ons.org

The complete article can be purchased for $24.95. All the profit from the purchase of the article goes to the Oncology Nursing Foundation for education and research of all oncology nurses to improve the mission of cancer care.

The reference link is below:

https://cjon.ons.org/cjon/23/3/patient-dignity-exploring-oncology-nurses-perceptions-during-end-life-care

Patient Dignity

Exploring oncology nurses' perceptions during end-of-life care

Barbara Crump, PhD, RN, NP-C, AOCNP®

BACKGROUND: Research on nurses' perceptions of dignity is limited, with most work instead focusing on patients' experiences. Maintaining the dignity of patients is considered to be an important element of nursing care; however, it is often diminished by the acts and omissions of healthcare providers.

OBJECTIVES: The purposes of this study were to understand oncology nurses' perceptions of care that supports patients' dignity during end-of-life hospitalization and to propose a theoretical foundation consistent with these perceptions as a guide to practice.

METHODS: A qualitative study using grounded theory was employed. Semistructured interviews with 11 experienced female oncology nurses generated insights into their perceptions of dignity in caring for terminally ill patients. Data were analyzed using the constant comparative method until data saturation was reached.

FINDINGS: This study revealed an emerging model for dignity care that uses communication, support, and facilitation in the education of nurses during end-of-life care. The proposed model could enhance the facilitation of nursing education and aid in the design of nursing course curricula and practical experiences that may improve nurses' ability to provide care supporting dignity.

KEYWORDS
dignity; nurse perceptions; end of life; terminal illness; patient care

DIGITAL OBJECT IDENTIFIER
10.1188/19.CJON.E46-E51

MAINTAINING THE DIGNITY OF PATIENTS IS IMPORTANT in the healthcare system (Lin, Watson, & Tsai, 2013). In the 21st century, providers of high-quality care, particularly palliative care, deem the dignity and respect of patients to be a necessary part of the care administered by nurses. Although research has shown that healthcare providers do not always maintain the dignity of patients during end-of-life care (Lin et al., 2013), limited knowledge exists regarding how oncology nurses believe the care they provide may support hospitalized patients' dignity at the end of life. Nurses have a central role in providing palliative and end-of-life care, and this includes helping people to die with dignity (Brown, Johnston, & Ostlund, 2011).

Dignity is a well-known concept in nursing. Sulmasy (2008) defined human dignity as having several positive aspects, including the feeling of self-worth, the belief in oneself, and the sense that others respect one's values. Preserving the dignity of the patient is one of the core concepts of nursing care, and a fundamental aspect of nursing practice is the respect for each patient's human rights, value, and dignity (American Nurses Association [ANA], 2015). Dignity during end-of-life care has become one of the most critical issues facing hospitalized patients. The emphasis on dignity in nursing reflects the professional nursing code of conduct (Matiti, Cotrel-Gibbons, & Teasdale, 2007). Care that ensures dignity offers patients honest communication about their disease, emotional support, and respect for their privacy (Lin & Tsai, 2011).

A study by Iranmanesh, Abbaszadeh, Dargahi, and Cheraghi (2009) involving 15 oncology nurses caring for patients at the end of life revealed that the nurses reported being attentive to the these terminally ill patients and their families by using humor, communicating through touch, and offering support. However, Matiti et al. (2007) reported that various barriers interfered with nurses caring for and maintaining the dignity of dying patients: nursing shortages, heavy workloads, and limited time for nurse-patient interactions. In spite of these obstacles, nurses demonstrated respect to each of the patients in their care through their skilled actions, which maintained patients' dignity (Matiti et al., 2007). Nurses have long provided their patients with dignity by respecting them and their privacy (Hegge, 2011).

Care that does not preserve dignity interferes with patients' recovery and decreases their quality of life (Watson, 2012). Nurses have faced a limited context that restricts individualized care, continuity, and primary contact, all of which limit patients' feeling of self-worth, leading to a potential loss of dignity. Although nurses and other healthcare providers possess knowledge and understanding of dignity, they cannot always apply it in practice (Näden & Eriksson, 2004). A review of the literature was important when discussing the topic of dignity in care because views expressed showed that patients' perceptions of dignity during care have not changed. For example, patients have often felt that healthcare providers compromise patients' personal dignity when administering care.

Background

Provision 1 of the ANA's (2015) nursing code of ethics states that "the nurse practices with compassion and respect for the inherent dignity, worth, and unique attributes of every person" (p. v). According to Milton (2008), nurses should validate patients as human beings by ensuring respect for their dignity. The nurse-patient relationship requires interpersonal attention, care, and certain relational qualities, such as the ability to sense patients' needs, which can be crucial in maintaining personal dignity (Nåden & Eriksson, 2004). Research on nurses' perceptions of dignity is limited, and the focus of past research seems limited to patients' experiences, not nurses' perceptions. Maintaining patients' dignity has been a defining characteristic of good nursing care since the time of Florence Nightingale, and it should be a quality indicator for measuring nurses' performance (Condon & Hegge, 2011).

Nightingale (1859) wrote in *Notes on Nursing* that nurses should be attentive to patients' well-being, needs, and response to treatment. Nightingale's focus was on providing patients with dignity and respect throughout the healing and dying process. According to Nightingale (1859), both a patient's body and his or her emotional attitudes were part of the observational assessment and the model from which nurses learned. Maintaining the dignity of patients is considered to be an important element

"Dignity during end-of-life care has become one of the most critical issues facing hospitalized patients."

of nursing care; however, it is often diminished by the acts and omissions of healthcare providers (Lin et al., 2013). Lin et al. (2013) note that heavy workloads and staff shortages adversely affect the provision of dignified care to patients. The demand for health care is increasing because of extended life expectancy and medical advances. The aforementioned barriers may prevent nurses from delivering dignified care and providing adequate privacy to patients (Lin et al., 2013). Although dignity may be difficult to define, many people agree that they know when they are not treated with dignity and respect (Meyer, 2010). What is less clear is how care that maintains dignity can be delivered when dignity is determined on an individual basis (Meyer, 2010). According to Coenen, Doorenbos, and Wilson (2007), dying patients and their families deserve nursing care that promotes dignity at the end of life. In this study, the inclusion of a postpositivist interpretive framework, exemplified in the systematic procedures of grounded theory developed by Corbin and Strauss (2008), may aid in understanding nurses' perceptions related to supporting the dignity of patients at the end of life during hospitalization.

This study sought to explore the following question: How do nurses perceive care that supports patients' dignity during hospitalization at the end of life? Accordingly, the purposes of this qualitative grounded study were (a) to understand oncology nurses' perceptions of care that supports patients' dignity during hospitalization at the end of life and (b) to propose a theoretical foundation consistent with these perceptions as a guide to practice. The research conducted in this study is the first step in developing a patient-centric model incorporating nurses' perceptions of end-of-life care that supports dignity for hospitalized patients.

Methods

The study was approved by the University of Phoenix Institutional Review Board, and all participants provided written informed consent. Semistructured interviews were conducted that employed questions derived from oncology nurses'

FIGURE 1.

PATIENT DIGNITY DURING END-OF-LIFE CARE INTERVIEW GUIDE

- What is your definition or perception of dignity?
- What are your perceptions of care that supports dignity?
- Do you remember an occasion when you felt you did not support patients' dignity?
- What strategies, if any, can healthcare leaders use to help nurses overcome barriers to providing care that supports dignity during the end of life?
- How would you support patients' dignity during end-of-life care?
- What do you think nurses do right to maintain the dignity of their patients during the end of life?
- What do nurses do poorly to maintain the dignity of their patients during end-of-life care?
- What barriers, if any, have you experienced when trying to deliver care that supported the dignity of your patients at the end of life?
- How would you facilitate dignity?

perceptions of dignity care at the end of life. The focus of this study included exploring the views of RNs from the Upstate New Jersey Oncology Nursing Society Chapter in an attempt to understand perceptions of care that support the dignity of hospitalized patients. Each interview lasted about 45 minutes, and the grounded theory approach (Corbin & Strauss, 2008) was used to gather enough information to reach saturation. The

interview guide was made up of nine questions related to the primary research question. Subinterview questions were developed that served to guide the data collection process.

Setting and Sample

For this qualitative study, participants were recruited from different hospitals in New Jersey. All participants (N = 11) were oncology

FIGURE 2.

SELECTED PARTICIPANT RESPONSES TO INTERVIEW QUESTIONS

WHAT IS YOUR DEFINITION OR PERCEPTION OF DIGNITY?
- "Being clean, giving support, honoring the wishes of the patients"
- "Being able to make one's own decision in a supportive environment"
- "Being treated as a human, showing respect for other[s] and getting respect in return"

WHAT ARE YOUR PERCEPTIONS OF CARE THAT SUPPORTS DIGNITY?
- "What is important to the patients . . . not being in pain, making sure the patient is clean and comfortable, meeting their needs, and, most of all, being present"
- "Physical comfort, care of the family, and meeting their emotional needs. . . . People who are dying, especially in the hospital . . . feel abandoned, and they need that relationship or connection."
- "Providing holistic care, not just taking care of a person's illness but the [whole] person—body, mind, and spirit"

DO YOU REMEMBER AN OCCASION WHEN YOU FELT YOU DID NOT SUPPORT PATIENTS' DIGNITY?
- "No, but feel [that] at time[s] patients' dignity can be compromised due to nurse burnout and high workload"
- "I think I could have done more, given more supportive information, speaking up for the patients—for example, when treatment compromised [the] patient's quality of life . . . or when the patient does not have enough information to make decision[s] related to end of life or treatment."
- "Yes—this is related to moral issues of the patient. [For] example, the patient and his family wanted everything done to keep him alive, even though he had terminal cancer. I didn't agree with their decision."

WHAT STRATEGIES, IF ANY, CAN HEALTHCARE LEADERS USE TO HELP NURSES OVERCOME BARRIERS TO PROVIDING CARE THAT SUPPORTS DIGNITY DURING THE END OF LIFE?
- "End-of-life care curriculum should be integrated into the nursing program; open communication with staff and patients [is needed], [including] the discussion of support needed for not only patients but also the family"
- "Support for nurses reduces [the] nurse–patient ratio, which will increase the time available to spend with the patient and most of all place value on . . . nurses."
- "Educate nurses in the importance of speaking up as a group."

HOW WOULD YOU SUPPORT PATIENTS' DIGNITY DURING END-OF-LIFE CARE?
- "By giving the best care possible, just being present and trying to meet all their needs, advocating for the need[s] of the patient"

- "Being supportive; making sure patients are clean and all symptoms related to the dying process are under control"
- "I would like to have the time to sit and listen to their stories."

WHAT DO YOU THINK NURSES DO RIGHT TO MAINTAIN THE DIGNITY OF THEIR PATIENTS DURING THE END OF LIFE?
- "They advocate for their patients, listen to their heartfelt stories; they wish they could spend more time with the patients."
- "I think nurses try to do all the right things to care for their patients, but the task of being a nurse tends to get in the way—for example, documentation, overwork, shortage of nursing staff, and mandatory overtime, which leads to burnout."
- "Nurses try to do what is right in caring for their patients, but there is limited time."

WHAT DO NURSES DO POORLY TO MAINTAIN THE DIGNITY OF THEIR PATIENTS DURING END-OF-LIFE CARE?
- "Nurses lack education in how to ask the right questions [and how to have] that conversation related to death, how to have the difficult conversation."
- "Nurses are so busy they forget patients are human; some nurses are caught [up] in completing the task, and they do not pay attention to . . . patient needs."
- "They do not have the time to spend with their patients; the job takes the nurses away from the bedside."

WHAT BARRIERS, IF ANY, HAVE YOU EXPERIENCED WHEN TRYING TO DELIVER CARE THAT SUPPORTED THE DIGNITY OF YOUR PATIENTS AT THE END OF LIFE?
- "Barriers can be the family [members] when they do not understand the dying process and disagree with the patient's wishes."
- "Lack of education in end-of-life care; nurses lack the understanding of the spiritual needs of the patients."
- "Nurses become burnt out due to overwork and massive amount of charting, which does not allow time to provide care that supports dignity"

HOW WOULD YOU FACILITATE DIGNITY?
- "Provide spas for the women . . . ensuring there is someone to take care of their hair, nails, and makeup"
- "Talk with each patient about his or her needs and what they expect, their goals of care."
- "Staff education, open communication, and workshop for nurses to discuss dignity and end-of-life care"

RNs with one or more years of experience caring for patients with advanced cancer. Three participants had 20 or more years of experience caring for patients at the end of life during hospitalization, with the remainder having 10 or fewer years of experience. Participants' ages ranged from 25 to 56 years, and all participants were oncology certified through the Oncology Nursing Certification Corporation.

Data Collection

A semistructured nine-question interview was used to guide data collection during the study (see Figure 1). The ninth question—"How would you facilitate dignity?"—opened up the discussion to include additional information provided by the participants. The data were obtained from 11 participants who discussed their personal perceptions during their interview (see Figure 2). Accommodating the participants and ensuring their privacy were important aspects of the research, with the participants choosing the time and location of the interview. More than half of the interviews were conducted in person, and the remaining interviews were conducted via telephone. A brief demographic questionnaire helped to capture information necessary to describe the sample. NVivo 10 was used for data analysis; throughout the transcription process, the current author reached out to the participants for clarification when needed. Data collection, coding, and analysis continued simultaneously throughout the study.

Data Analysis and Synthesis

Codes (words or groups of words taken verbatim from participants during interviews) were used to create categories for each new idea. If the codes were similar, they were grouped together as concepts. Constant comparison of concepts facilitated construction of the theoretical framework. The analytical process included coding, writing, and note-taking. The open-coding process began with an exploration of experiences of how nurses support patients' dignity during hospitalization at the end of life. Nodes were identified to facilitate the use of NVivo 10 techniques to create the categories derived from coding to reveal patterns and themes about care that supports dignity during the end of life. Through open codes, a list of emerging categories was identified, which aided in understanding participants' perceptions of care that supports their dignity during hospitalization at the end of life. Another important strategy for analyzing the data involved reviewing the frequency of keywords in the categories. Through axial coding, the current author discovered links between categories and concepts identified through the open-coding process. The evolving relationships were validated, and the categories were filled in for refinement. Open coding from data analysis was selected for each interview question.

Results

Data analysis identified three pairs of major categories—communication, facilitation, and support—and several subcategories. Subcategories identified were as follows: listening, being present,

building a relationship, advocate, honoring wishes, education, in-service sessions, workshops, course curriculum, physical needs, emotional support, compassion, respect, and treated as human. Figure 3 highlights the three major categories and their subcategories that are tied to the development of an emergent model for care that supports dignity, based on study participants' perceptions; these will be refined through additional testing and studies. A combination of these factors contributes to delivering care that supports the dignity of patients during the end of life. According to the participants in the current study, an environment that inspires and enhances patients' dignity must be created to ensure dignity during end of life.

Rationale for Proposed Model

COMMUNICATION: Care that ensures dignity offers patients choices, honest communication about the disease and its

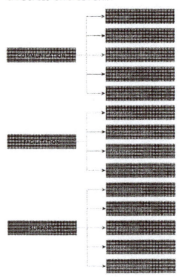

FIGURE 3.

CATEGORIES AND SUBCATEGORIES FOR EMERGENT MODEL OF DIGNITY-ENHANCING CARE BASED ON STUDY DATA

PATIENT DIGNITY

treatment, emotional support, and respect for privacy (Lin & Tsai, 2011). Participants noted the importance of nurses being able to advocate for the personal wishes of patients who are unable to speak for themselves. The emergent categories suggest the importance of nurses being present to listen to patients' personal stories and concerns and to build relationships with patients and their families through effective communication.

FACILITATION: Participants noted that nurses lacked the education needed to provide hospitalized patients with care to support their dignity at the end of life. Discussions indicated the importance of nurses having an undergraduate-level course with an inpatient clinical component that focuses on end-of-life care. Participants recommended workshops that allow time for self-reflection on and discussion of delivering care that supports dignity. They also indicated the importance of mandatory in-service sessions on end-of-life care for all staff caring for patients during this critical period. The proposed model may be used to guide nursing leaders and educators in the facilitation of care that supports dignity from participants' perspectives; this could include workshops and course curricula with practical experience that may be able to improve nurses' and students' ability to provide care supporting dignity at the end of life.

SUPPORT: Participants noted that end-of-life care that supports the dignity of hospitalized patients comprises many factors. The most important of these factors were treating patients as human beings, giving patients respect, providing patients with physical comfort and emotional support, and honoring patients' wishes, whatever they were (e.g., empowering patients' family members to stay at the bedside, finding a place where patients can spend quality time with their pets, building trusting relationships with patients, returning to the bedside as promised). The participants also noted that nurse leaders are not always supportive of nurses. The participants stated that nurse leaders can lead the journey toward delivering care that supports patient dignity by showing compassion to staff and decreasing workload so that nurses have the time needed to spend with patients.

Discussion

Based on the results of this study, it is suggested that educational workshops and in-service sessions be incorporated into units to allow nurses to reflect on dignity and the care that is needed to support patients at the end of life. In addition, the implementation of education in the undergraduate nursing curricula that is centered on end-of-life care and has a clinical focus could help to empower nurse sensitivity related to caring for the whole person rather than emphasize task-based care for patients who are terminally ill. Nursing leaders also could promote patient dignity by developing a culture of mentoring to aid nurses in delivering care that supports the dignity of patients.

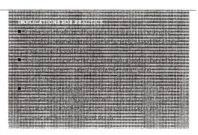

Limitations

Limitations of this study included its qualitative methodology, which may be affected by researcher bias, and the focus on patients with cancer and the small sample size, which may limit generalizability of the findings.

Conclusion

The purposes of this qualitative grounded study were to understand nurses' perceptions of care that supports patients' dignity during hospitalization at the end of life and to propose a theoretical foundation as a guide to practice. The inclusion of a postpositivist interpretive framework, exemplified in the systematic procedures of grounded theory developed by Corbin and Strauss (2008), helped to underscore the nurses' perceptions of care that supports dignity during the end of life. The interviews with 11 oncology RNs with one or more years of experience in caring for patients with advanced cancer led to distinctive codes and revealed categories and subcategories. The findings of this study suggest that a theory that uses communication, facilitation in the education of nurses in end-of-life care, and support may enhance the communication process and lead to the delivery of care that supports the dignity of hospitalized patients at the end of life. These findings serve in the expansion of knowledge and further theory development in this area and offer value to nurses caring for patients with terminal illnesses other than advanced cancer.

Barbara Crump, PhD, RN, NP-C, AOCNP®, is an assistant professor in the School of Nursing at Felician University in Lodi, NJ. Crump can be reached at crumpb@ felician.edu, with copy to CJONEditor@ons.org. (Submitted April 2018. Accepted December 20, 2018.)

The author takes full responsibility for this content and did not receive honoraria or disclose any relevant financial relationships. The article has been reviewed by independent peer reviewers to ensure that it is objective and free from bias.

REFERENCES

American Nurses Association. (2015). *Code of ethics for nurses with interpretive statements*. Silver Spring, MD: Author.

Brown, H., Johnston, B., & Ostlund, U. (2011). Identifying care actions to conserve dignity in end-of-life care. *British Journal of Community Nursing, 16*, 238–245.

Coenen, A., Doorenbos, A.Z., & Wilson, S.A. (2007). Nursing interventions to promote dignified

87

From GED to Ph.D.

ABOUT THE AUTHOR
BARBARA V. CRUMP

I plan to continue my research by developing a model for end-of-life care and looking into ways to implement the model. This issue became particularly relevant when my mother became ill. I took care of her at home with hospice, making sure she had first-rate, quality care and had the family around her as this was extremely important. Nobody should suffer at their end-of-life. Dignity and respect should be maintained during this time in one's life. Yes, we have hospice, but that can be a struggle. *How do we make it better?*

Recently, I started a nursing scholarship in the Crump Family name for African American students at William Paterson University. The annual scholarship shall be awarded for the purpose of empowering African American nursing students in dignity care at the end-of-life.

For Further Information,
Email: barbaracrump@aol.com.